Fragments Of Us:
बिखरे पल

A Journey Through Love's Remains

P.K. Artha

Made with ♥ on the BookLeaf Publishing Platform
www.bookleafpub.in
www.bookleafpub.com

Dedication

"For the ones who were, who are, and who could have been.
For the moments that slipped away, but left their echoes behind."

Preface

Dear Reader,
Some stories are lived, some are left behind, and some remain unfinished—lingering in the spaces between words, in the silence after a conversation, in the moments that never turned into memories.
This book is a collection of such moments. A journey through love, longing, loss, and the quiet realizations that shape us. It is not just poetry; it is the voice of everything unsaid. Some lines might remind you of someone, some might make you pause, and some might whisper the words you always wanted to hear.

Each poem is written in both Hindi and English, because emotions have no language—they only have feelings. You can read them in any order, but if you follow them one after another, you might notice a story hidden within.
I hope these words find a home in your heart.
With love,
P.K. Artha

Acknowledgements

This book wouldn't have been possible without the people
who became poetry in my life.
To the moments that inspired these verses—thank you
for existing, even if only for a while.
To my family and friends—thank you for always believing
in my words, even when I didn't.

And to you, the reader—thank you for holding these
fragments of me in your hands. I hope you find a piece of
yourself in them too.

- P.K. Artha

The Beginning - शुरुआत

An odd encounter, a smile,
A fresh echo in some corner of the heart.
What was in your eyes,
Was never heard anywhere else.
The season was like a new song,
Filled only with the essence of being with you.
The things we discussed as we strolled,
Still reside in the journey of memories.

एक अजनबी मुलाक़ात, एक मुस्कुराहट,
दिल के किसी कोने में एक नई आहट।
तेरी आँखों में जो बात थी,
वो कहीं और कभी सुनाई ना दी।
मौसम भी जैसे एक नया गीत गाया,
जिसमे सिर्फ तेरे साथ का एहसास समाया।
चलते चलते जो बातें होती थीं,
आज भी यादों के सफर में बसी है।

Stories in the Eyes - आँखों में कहानियाँ

Your radiance, like the light within the eyes,
I was lost, like in a maze.
Stories were composed in those deep eyes,
Without words, they communicated a thousand words.
Even during the night when it is dark, they glowed,
As if they were a special part of my life.
To behold my story in your eyes,
Had become my biggest habit.

तेरी आँखों का नूर, एक रोशनी की तरह,
मैं खो गया था, जैसा कोई राह फराह।
कहानियाँ लिखी थी उन गहरी आँखों में,
एक शब्द भी कहे बिना, सब कह दिया था इन्हों ने।
रात के अँधेरों में भी वो चमक रही थी,
जैसे मेरी जिंदगी का सिर्फ एक मखसूस हिसा बनी थी।
तेरी आँखों में अपनी कहानी देखना,
मेरी सबसे बड़ी आदत बन चुकी थी।

The Paths - रास्ते

Do we go one by one or go together?
Stay with you or take another path?
The paths are difficult, the heart doesn't understand,
Whether to reach you or forget myself, the mystery
remains unsolved.
Relationships are never straightforward, they're in some
sort of strange haze,
And we keep searching for each other.

एक साथ चालू या अलग मोड़ ले लूं,
तेरे साथ रह कर या किसी और मोड़ पर हो लूं।
रास्ते मुश्किल हैं, दिल समझ नहीं पाता,
तुझ तक पहुंचूं या खुद को भूल जाऊं, ये राज़ नहीं खुल पाता।
रिश्ते कभी साफ नहीं होते, वो एक अजीब से धुंध में होते हैं,
और हम बस एक दूसरे को ढूंढते रहते हैं।

Nameless Bond - बेनाम रिश्ता

No word of love, no act of friendliness,
But not every second passes without you.
There was something strange in this relationship,
But without you, it is empty.
In the late hours of night, when I am sitting in solitude,
Only you appear amidst the restlessness.
The relationship that was present without words,
Today, it's found written in the book of memories.

ना मोहब्बत का दावा, ना दोस्ती का वास्ता,
फिर भी हर पल तेरे बिना अधूरा लगता।
एक अजनबीयात थी इस रिश्ते में,
फिर भी तेरे बिना सब सुना लगता।
रात के आखिरी पहर में, जब तन्हा बैठता हूँ,
सिर्फ तू ही दिखती है, बेचैनियों के दरमियान।
जो रिश्ता शब्द बिना जीता था,
आज वो यादों की किताब में लिखा है

Evening Lights - शाम के उजाले

That night spent with you,
Its light continues to radiate in my heart.
And in the silence, there were words,
Your laughter still rings through in the winds.
Sitting on a bench, bewildered in the glow of city lights,
All the feelings of the present are still there in my eyes.
You were telling me something, but not verbally,
Your face became the deepest page of my book.

वो शाम जो तेरे साथ बितायी थी,
आज भी उसकी रोशनी मेरे दिल को चमकती है।
खामोशियों में भी बातें थीं,
तेरी हंसी अब भी हवाओं में गूंजती है।
एक बेंच पर बैठे, शहर की रोशनी में खो गये थे,
उस दोस्त का हर एहसास अब भी आँखों में बसा है।
तू कह रही थी कुछ, पर शब्दों से नहीं,
तेरा चेहरा ही मेरी किताब का सबसे गहरा पन्ना बन गया था।

The Heart's Gathering - दिल की महफ़िल

The heart's assembly was graced only with you,
Without words, this body spoke volumes.
For an instant, we had it all,
But we were still strangers—what sort of dream was
this?
Your smile was the morning of my love,
And your memories, the final light of the night.
Each day that passes with you,
Still adorns my heart like a gathering.

दिल की महफिल सजती थी सिर्फ तेरे संग,
बिना कहे सब कह जाता था ये अंग।
एक पल में सब कुछ था अपना,
फिर भी हम रहे अजनबी, ये क्या सपना?
तेरी हंसी मेरी मोहब्बत की सुबह थी,
और तेरी यादें, शाम का आखिरी उजाला।
हर दिन जो तेरे साथ था,
वो आज भी मेरे दिल में एक महफ़िल की तरह सजता है।

Unspoken Desires - ख्वाहिशें

There was but one yearning in the far corner of the
heart,
A desire to make you my own.
But time changed the paths,
And we were confined to memories.
Each turn of events had a unique outcome,
But without you, it was an unfinished story.
Dreams never work out,
They remain as a secret in the heart's corner.

दिल के एक कोने में, बस एक ख्वाहिश थी,
तुझको अपना कहने की एक गुजारिश थी।
पर वक़्त ने रास्ते बदल दिये,
और हम सिर्फ यादों में सिमट गए।
जिंदगी का हर मोड़ एक नया नतिजा लाया,
पर तेरे बिना वो एक अधूरा अफ़साना बन गया।
ख्वाहिशें कभी पूरी नहीं होती,
वो सिर्फ दिल के कोने में बस एक राज़ की तरह रहती है।

That Day - वो दिन

The day it all turned around,
Your words, your tone, all faded away.
The light that in your eyes,
In a moment, it dimmed.
What was mine a moment ago,
A moment later, it felt like someone else's.

वो दिन जब सब बदल गया,
तेरी बातें, तेरा लहजा, सब ढल गया।
आँखों में जो रोशनी थी,
एक पल में वो धुँधला गया।
एक पल पहले जो सब कुछ अपना लगता था,
एक पल बाद वो सब पराया हो गया।

Unsent Letters - चिट्ठियां

The sheets of paper, once penned for you,
Still conceal the same hurt.
The words I could not speak,
Were concealed in each word.
Love never required words,
But finally, we never said it.

कागज़ के पन्ने, जो कभी तुझे लिखे थे,
आज भी उनमें वही दुख छिपा है।
शब्दों में जो बात कह नहीं पाया,
वो हर हर्फ में कहीं छुपी रह गई है।
मोहब्बत कभी शब्दों की मोहताज नहीं थी,
लेकिन अफसोस, हमने उसका इस्तेमाल नहीं किया।

Time - वक़्त

Time altered everything,
Your smile, your voice.
The vow to walk hand in hand,
Became a tale.
But memories do not change with time,
They deepen.

वक़्त ने सब बदल दिया,
तेरी हंसी भी, तेरी बातें भी.
जो कभी साथ चलने की कसम थी,
वो सिर्फ एक कहानी बन कर रह गई।
पर वक़्त के साथ यादें नहीं बदलती,
वो बस और गहरी हो जाती हैं

The Unfinished Story - अधूरी कहानी

Were we merely a tale?
That started but never concluded.
Was there an absence of total love,
Or did we not allow it to conclude.
I'm living without you,
But living with you had a different charm.

क्या हम सिर्फ एक कहानी ही रह गए?
जो शुरू तो हुई थी, पर कभी ख़तम नहीं हुई।
एक मुकम्मल मोहब्बत की कमी थी,
हां शायद हमने ही उसे मुकम्मल नहीं होने दिया।
तेरे बिना भी मैं जी रहा हूँ,
पर तेरे साथ जीने का मजा ही अलग था।

Shadows - साये

Your memories are like shadows,
That stay with me in the light,
But grow deeper in the darkness.
The moments spent only with you,
Now appear on every path.
I'm walking,
But the shadows never leave.

तेरी यादें साये की तरह हैं,
जो रोशनी में साथ रहती है,
पर अँधेरों में और गहरी हो जाती हैं।
जो पल सिर्फ तेरे साथ बिताये थे,
आज वो हर रास्ते पर दिखते हैं।
मैं चल रहा हूँ,
पर साये कभी पीछा नहीं छोड़ते।

Conversations in the Wind - हवाओ से बातें

I've learned to talk to the winds,
Because you don't listen anymore.
The wind takes away my questions,
And the answers never return.
The words I couldn't say to you,
I'm living by saying them to myself.

हवाओ से बातें करना सीख लिया है,
क्योंकि अब तू सुनती नहीं.
मेरे सवाल हवा ले जाती है,
और जवाब कभी वापस नहीं आता.
जो बातें तुझसे कह नहीं पाया,
आज वो खुद से कह कर जी रहा हूं।

Passing By - रहगुज़र

I saw you again,
On a busy street, for a moment.
The same face, the same eyes,
But perhaps you are no longer the same.
Or maybe I am not,
Who never knew what it was like to exist without you.

तुझे एक बार फिर देखा मैंने,
एक भिड़ भरी सड़क पे, एक पल के लिए।
वही चेहरा, वही आँखें,
पर शायद अब तू वो नहीं रही जो पहले थी।
हां शायद मैं भी वही नहीं रहा,
जो तेरे बिना जीना नहीं जानता था.

Falling Star - टूटा सितारा

Love is also a falling star,
That is only apparent while it's in free fall.
Something that had been part of life,
Now only lives in memory.
The moonlight isn't so deep,
As the sorrowful memories of love.

मोहब्बत भी एक टूटा सितारा ही है,
जिसे सिर्फ गिरते वक्त देखा जा सकता है।
जो कभी जिंदगी का हिसा थी,
वो अब सिर्फ एक याद बनके जीती है।
चाँद की रोशनी भी उतनी गहरी नहीं,
जितनी मोहब्बत की दुख भरी यादें होती हैं।

Come Back Someday - लौट आना

If you ever have to come back, give me a shout,
I'll be right where you left me.
The same unresolved tale,
The same incomplete person.
But even if you do return,
Maybe we will not be the same from then on.

अगर कभी लौटना हो, तो बता देना,
मैं वही रहूंगा, जहां तू छोड़ गई थी।
वही अधूरी कहानी,
वही अधूरा इंसान।
पर अगर लौट भी आये,
तो शायद हम वैसे नहीं होंगे, जैसे थे।

The Last Meeting - आखिरी मुलाकात

Do you remember the last time we got together?
My eyes asked questions,
And your lips had silence.
What I meant to say, I could not,
And what I said, lost its meaning.
Sometimes love feels better,
In silence, not in words.

वो दिन याद है जब हम आखिरी बार मिले थे?
मेरी आँखों में सवाल थे,
और तेरे होठों पे चुप।
जो कहना था, कह नहीं पाया,
और जो कह दिया, उसका मतलब ही नहीं रहा।
मोहब्बत कभी कभी कहने से ज़्यादा,
चुप रहने में बेहतर लगती है।

A New Journey - नया सफ़र

I was not used to walking without you,
But now the paths give me peace alone.
What was right only with you,
Now feels better with myself too.
It is not everything that love is,
Sometimes it's about discovering yourself.

तेरे बिना चलने की आदत नहीं थी,
पर अब रास्ते अकेले भी सुकून देते हैं।
पहले जो सिर्फ तेरे साथ अच्छा लगता था,
अब वो खुद के साथ भी बेहतर लगता है।
मोहब्बत सिर्फ किसी के साथ जीने का नाम नहीं,
कभी-कभी खुद को पाने का भी नाम है।

The City of Memories - यादों का शहर

The city does not change, the roads do not change,
We ourselves have altered.
The place that was formerly ours,
Now feels strange.
But memories don't go anywhere,
They are hidden in every single back alley of the city.

शहर वही है, रास्ते वही हैं,
बस हम बदल गये हैं.
जो जगह कभी अपनी लगती थी,
आज वही अजनबी सी लगती है.
पर यादें कहीं नहीं जाती,
वो शहर की हर गली में छुपी रहती है।

Beyond Words - शब्दों से परे

Some emotions cannot be described,
As one of those timeless songs that still touches the
heart,
Such as a short encounter which is remembered for life.
Love is such a story as well,
Where outside and beyond the spoken words,
The words unspoken are meaningful.

कुछ एहसास शब्दों से परे होते हैं,
जैसा एक पुराना गीत, जो अब भी दिल को छू जाता है।
जैसी एक छोटी सी मुलाकात, जो जिंदगी भर याद रहती है।
मोहब्बत भी एक ऐसी कहानी है,
जिस्मे हर शब्द से ज्यादा,
वो बातें मायने रखती हैं जो कभी कहीं ही नहीं गई।

The Paths (Epilogue) - रास्ते

And so ends this journey,
Or maybe it's merely the beginning of a new journey.
Love isn't a destination,
But a journey for a lifetime, though.
Sometimes separation is unavoidable,
Because every tale needs a conclusion.

और ये सफर यहीं ख़तम होता है,
हां शायद ये सिर्फ एक नए रास्ते की शुरुआत है।
मोहब्बत एक मंजिल नहीं,
बाल्की एक सफर है जो जिंदगी भर चलता है।
कहीं कभी बिछड़ना भी जरूरी होता है,
क्योंकि हर कहानी का एक अंजाम जरूरी है।